Seeds and Soil

Bernadette Brexel

Rosen REAL READERS

Rosen Classroom™
New York

I plant a seed.

A seed needs soil.

Soil helps a seed grow.

A seed turns into a plant.

A plant needs water.

This plant is ready to eat.

Words To Know

plant

seed

soil

water